COSMIC!

LEICESTER VOL I

Edited by Simon Harwin

First published in Great Britain in 1999 by
POETRY NOW YOUNG WRITERS
1-2 Wainman Road, Woodston,
Peterborough, PE2 7BU
Telephone (01733) 230748

HB ISBN 0 75430 257 1
SB ISBN 0 75430 258 X

FOREWORD

With over 63,000 entries for this year's Cosmic competition, it has proved to be our most demanding editing year to date.

We were, however, helped immensely by the fantastic standard of entries we received, and, on behalf of the Young Writers team, thank you.

Cosmic Leicester Vol I is a tremendous reflection on the writing abilities of 8 & 9 year old children, and the teachers who have encouraged them must take a great deal of credit.

We hope that you enjoy reading *Cosmic Leicester Vol I* and that you are impressed with the variety of poems and style with which they are written, giving an insight into the minds of young children and what they think about the world today.

CONTENTS

Hetal Pala	64
Jiten Anand	64
Fatima Hussein	65
Afra Osman	65
Veekash & Kisan Umrania	66
Neha Karia	66
Priten Thakrar	66
Vandana Lad	67
Tejasvi Sankada	67
Sona Nathwani	68
Bhakti Makwana	68
Daniel Stewart-Dexter	68
Sonam Chagger	69
Nabeel Boliya	69
Chirag V Limbachia	70

Millfield Primary School

Kyla Archer	70
Claire Graham	71
Joseph Byland	71
Sarah Naish	72
Natalie Carr	72
Anoushka Kansara	73
Dionne Lawrence	73
Fiona Brakes	74

Old Mill Primary School

Kate Conaron	74
Rachael Knappier	75
Arron Mee	75
Victoria Lucas	76
Phoebe Blockley Campton	76
Sam Lee	77
Michaela Gibbins	77
Natalie Harris	77
Lucy Bass	78

Michael Milner	78
Nathan Underhill	78
Emma Marfleet	79
Shaun Parsons	79
Jonathan Taylor	80
Sharon Scarborough	80
Joe Needham	80
Anne-Marie Adamson	81
Ellie George Preson	81

Overdale Junior School

Charlie Patel	81
Pawan Sharma	82
Jaskiren Loyal	82
Rosie Henderson	83
Nikesh Patel	83
James Burnage	84
Gemma Mcfarlane	84
Alice Pott-Negrine	85
Gurpreet Kaur Deol	85
Chris Pollard	86
Martin Sanderson	86
Chad Allen	87
Luca Jordan	87
Claire Hannon	88
Tom Gill	88
Emma Fox	88
Laurie Bennett	89
Joe Stewart	89
Belinda Kaur Basra	90
Natalie Allen	90
Sarena Kaur Rai	91

Rushey Mead Primary School

Prashant K Asher	91
Jemini Vaghela	92
Divya Gosai	92
Aarti Sonigra	93

THE POEMS

RIVERS

River, river, fast river.
Rivers go too fast.
The river is going,
splash,
crash,
zoom,
whiz.
It slows down,
still spitting and splashing.
It's nearly
reached the ocean.
Spreading out.
The sea animals
have new water.

Nathan Torr (8)
Braunstone Frith Junior School

THE ANDERSON SHELTER

Down in the Anderson shelter,
where nobody knows,
It's cold, dark,
smelly and damp.
It's wet.
It's hard.
It's scary and frightening.
It's small.
I hate Anderson shelters.

Jamie Tarbert (9)
Braunstone Frith Junior School

I KNOW SOMEONE

I know someone who can
jump as far as a frog.

I know someone who can
touch their wrist with their thumb.

I know someone who can
run with an egg.

I know someone who can
whistle like a bird.

I know someone who can
swim like a fish.

I know someone who can
sit down on their head.

I know someone who can
walk on their knees.

I know someone who can
write as fast as a computer
and that someone is
Me!

Naomi Jackson (9)
Braunstone Frith Junior School

THE ROBBER

The robber robbed a ruby-red robin,
A ruby-red robin the robber robbed.
Where is the ruby-red robin the robber robbed?

Alex Gray (9)
Braunstone Frith Junior School

THE RIVER

Crashing, splashing down the hill,
It's still fast
Zooming, splashing, bubbling.
Other rivers joining on.
It's going steady.
Look!
It meanders
Curling, swirling, twirling, twisting.
It's deep.
It's ending soon. Here comes the mouth.
Into the sea.

Jade Allen (8)
Braunstone Frith Junior School

WHAT IS RED?

Red is a ladybird
All bright and clean.
Red is a rose
That I have seen.

Red is the best
Colour of all.
When I'm in the pool
I play with my red rubber ball.

Simon Henfrey (9)
Braunstone Frith Junior School

THE RIVER

Far away a mountain stands,
I hear the river far.
I feel the rain,
I see the water,
Zooming down the waterfall.
I feel a shiver down my back.
It comes to an end.
I say goodbye to the waterfall.
Goodbye!

Holly Harris (9)
Braunstone Frith Junior School

CATHERINE WHEEL

Catherine wheels
Go round and round,
Sizzle and fizzle
And touch the ground!

Alicia Paget (9)
Braunstone Frith Junior School

SPIDERS

Hairy spiders walk on their web.
Scary spiders crawl in the bath.
Fat spiders crawl in my shoes.
Money spiders climb on my head.
Big spiders go in my bed!

Matthew Buckley (9)
Braunstone Frith Junior School

THE JOURNEY OF A RIVER

The fast flowing river
comes from the mountains.
The journey has started.
The dangerous river crashes down.
Waits for no one.
Very violent.
Hitting and crashing,
knocking down trees.
It's slowing down.
The river's meandering as it goes down.
Takes a short oxbow lake.
The water's cold,
it makes me shiver.
It slows down,
getting deeper and deeper.
Rippling river,
not very fast.
The journey has ended at last.

Lyle Webster (9)
Braunstone Frith Junior School

BONFIRE NIGHT

Will you watch the rocket zoom into the sky?
Will you watch the rocket go bang and explode?
Will you watch the rocket go bash into a hot sun
And sizzle up like a sausage?
Will you watch it come back down again?

Emma Winder (8)
Braunstone Frith Junior School

I KNOW SOMEONE

I know someone who can
count up to ten in one second.

I know someone who can
swallow fifteen fruit pastels
in one go.

I know someone who can
put their finger
all the way down their throat.

I know someone who can
pop their eyes right out.

I know someone who can
make their tongue
touch their nose
and that someone is
Me!

Aisha Blake (9)
Braunstone Frith Junior School

ROCKET

Rocket clashes
Rocket flashes
Rocket goes up in the air.
I wish I could hold one
Then I could go up to the moon!

Nikesh Chavda (9)
Braunstone Frith Junior School

FIREWORKS

Fireworks crackle,
Fireworks spin,
Fireworks end up falling in.
I can see a rocket
Flying in the air.
I can see fireworks flying everywhere.
There are bangs, crashes at night,
And they're just all right.
When it's time to go to bed,
I dream about fireworks,
They're in my head.

Emma Whitmore (8)
Braunstone Frith Junior School

THE RIVER

Splashing, crashing all around
Makes me shiver all the time.
Frothy, racing round the bend,
Zooming, whizzing, spitting now.
Getting deeper as it goes down,
Slow, slower calming down.
Wider, weaker, harmless,
Deeper, rippling down
As it goes into the sea.

Rachael Boye
Braunstone Frith Junior School

WHAT IS YELLOW?

Yellow is the sun,
shining in the sky.
Yellow is a beautiful sunflower.
Yellow is a car,
driving in the street.
Yellow is a beautiful buttercup.
Yellow is a jumper,
nice and woolly.
Yellow is a beautiful daffodil.
Yellow is a pencil
to colour with.
Yellow is a basket
to put things in.

Samantha Gutteridge (9)
Braunstone Frith Junior School

HARVEST

H arvest is good, harvest is good.
A pples are sweet and very ripe.
R ed roses smell lovely.
V egetables are so ripe.
E at fruits, they are good for you.
S trawberries are sweet.
T ractors cut the corn.

Roxanne Featherstone
Braunstone Frith Junior School

THE RIVER'S JOURNEY

The beginning of the river,
Zooming, fast.
Crashing and spitting
as the mountain stands.
Whizzing, splashing
Crashing on the rocks.
Calming down a bit.
Getting very wavy.
Chipping, meandering
Getting slower,
wider,
weaker,
deeper.
Ending in the sea.

Rhea Brant (9)
Braunstone Frith Junior School

THE RIVER'S JOURNEY

The river is fast and strong
when I see it going along.
The river is crashing
when I see it dashing.
The river is spitting
when I see it whizzing.
The river is weak
when it is getting deep.

Zoe Turner (8)
Braunstone Frith Junior School

AIR RAID SHELTERS

I love Anderson shelters.
They are so loud,
and there's always a great big crowd.

I love Anderson shelters.
They are small.
But let me tell you,
they are not that tall.

I love Anderson shelters.
They are damp and noisy,
wet and smelly.
But I wish they had tellies.

I love Anderson shelters.
They're cold, draughty and grotty.
But I love Anderson shelters.

James Angrave (9)
Braunstone Frith Junior School

DARKNESS

Darkness comes, darkness goes,
Children are afraid at night.
Shadows are cast upon your wall
While noises are about.
Darkness gradually builds up and up,
While the world gently sleeps.

Stacey Benstead (10)
Braunstone Frith Junior School

SPIDERS

Small spiders run
down the plughole.
Big spiders run quickly
in the bath.
Scary spiders run
up the window.
Big spiders creep
in the bedroom.
Horrible spiders run
on the ground.
Scary spiders make webs
in the garden.
Big spiders crawl
in the grass.

Stacey Atkin (9)
Braunstone Frith Junior School

THE JOURNEY OF THE RIVER

The river comes hurtling
Down the mountain slope.
Violent as anything.
Powerful, strong, speeding, fast, thin.
Racing, zooming, frothy, whizzing.
Getting slower
Calming down.
Meandering, chipping.
Going down a waterfall.
Getting wider.
Leaves an oxbow lake
Ending in the sea.

Alison Bates (8)
Braunstone Frith Junior School

CATS GO ANYWHERE

Cats go anywhere,
Up the chimney
On a chair,
On your head,
In your bed,
Chase mice,
Sugar and spice.
Cats go anywhere.

Jo Mackness (8)
Braunstone Frith Junior School

IF I WERE

If I were a teddy
I'd live in a town.

If I were a horse
I'd gallop a course.

If I were a whale
I'd fight a gale.

If I were a monkey
I'd live in a hall.

If I were a person
I'd eat my tuck.

If I were a diver
I'd look before I went.

If I were a cat
I'd be so fat.

Charlotte Manley (8)
Danemill CP School

WHAT'S THAT SOUND?

Crackle, whistle, whoosh, bang!
Isn't that a strange sound.
Let's see if I can work it out.
Crackle sounds like a bonfire.
Whistle, whoosh, bang!
I think I know what it might be.
Fireworks perhaps?

Clip, clop, clip, clop!
What could that sound be?
I'll try and work it out.
1, 2, 3 Ah! I think I know now,
It sounds like a horse.
Why don't I look out the window and see.

Tick-tock, tick-tock, what could it be?
It sounds like it's very close to me.
I'll have a look and see.
Ah! Now I know it's right next to me.
It's my alarm clock, now I see.

Victoria Courtney (9)
Danemill CP School

POETRY

G is for girl-power
I   is for I like the Spice Girls
R is for rich and poor
L is for the lucky rich people
S is for the Spice Girls.

Anisha Saund (9)
Danemill CP School

IF I WERE

If I were a bumblebee I would fly around collecting pollen
Then I would go back home and make some yummy honey.

If I were a ladybird I would crawl around all day
But I would have to dodge out of the way when a human came my way.

If I were a butterfly I would fly around
Every day I would show my wings off.

If I were a grasshopper I would hop around all day
If a human came too close, I would hop out of the way.

Gemma Astill (9)
Danemill CP School

SNACKER

Snacker is a wizard
Maybe wizard of the world
He sings sometimes in the morning
And sets fire to his hat.
He likes to have a sleep
He'll sleep all the day
And be awake all the night.
Sometimes people call him
The Owler Wizard.
He likes to make potions.
But not anymore
I've just heard him
Going bonkers about a potion.

Alan Potter (8)
Danemill CP School

IF I WERE

If I were a spider
creeping around the house
I'd have to be very quiet
creeping round the house.

If I were a butterfly
flying through the sky
everyone would look at me
flying through the sky.

If I were a ladybird
crawling in the garden
I would crawl and crawl
all day long.

If I were a bumblebee
I would collect all the pollen
then fly back home.

Carla Starmer (9)
Danemill CP School

IF I WERE A CHEETAH

If I were a cheetah
I would be faster than you
I would be the king of speed
And then I would have to feed all the cubs.
I would be in the safari park every week.
I would be climbing up the tree.

Stuart Iddisah (8)
Danemill CP School

IF I WERE

If I were a brick
I'd be worn out quick
My mum said I wouldn't like it a bit.

If I were wood
I'd be so good
But I'd rot so quick and that is that.

If I were an elastic band
I'd snap at everyone
Beside that, I would snap.

If I were some glass
I'd be so cold
But the wind would smash me.

I'd like to be a clay pot
I wouldn't like it though
Because it would smell a lot.

I suppose I'd like to be myself
And that is that.

Thomas Tollafield (8)
Danemill CP School

MY PET DOG

My pet dog,
Barks very loud,
She wags her tail,
Like a whip.

Bark, bark, bark,
Very loud,
Drives the people,
Out of their minds.

Whip, whip, whip,
The bad people,
Drives the people,
Out of the town.

My pet dog,
Is always bad,
Come on,
Let's go to the park.

Rachel Chan (8)
Danemill CP School

PIG POEM

There once was a pig.
He danced to a wonderful jig.
He wears the most wonderful wig.

He has four legs,
Which are made of brown pegs.
This old pig has only two pegs.
So he begs and begs for more of these pegs.
For two more legs.

He has a pink snout.
To eat big amounts.
With his wonderful snout.

Amy Strong (8)
Danemill CP School

WALKING IN THE JUNGLE

Walking in the jungle
What did I see?
A little baby monkey laughing at me.

Walking in the jungle
What did I see?
A lion roaring at me.

Walking in the jungle
What did I see?
A snake hissing at me.

Walking in the jungle
What did I see?
A beautiful path waiting for me.

Sebastian Chapman (9)
Danemill CP School

THE LIFE OF A SEWER RAT

I have seen a little rat
he looks very fat.
He was going down a drain
he must have felt a pain.
When he got in the sewers
his friends said 'Come to us.'
They all went to a flat,
mouse, hamster and rat.
And that is the life of a sewer rat.

Richard Todd (9)
Danemill CP School

MY MICE

I have got some mice
But they don't like rice.
They would think about their wife
Whilst getting a life.

All my mice fight
One always gets a bite.
And nearly dies with fright
But always ends up alright.

The problem came after that
My brother got a cat.
The cat messed with my mice
And ate them in a trice.

Then I cried and cried
Because my mice had died.
Then I sighed
But oh dear never mind.

Craig Jones (9)
Danemill CP School

COLOURS

The sky is blue
So are you
Rain is too.
And when you are cold
So is ice.
And water too.

Thomas Wilson (9)
Danemill CP School

IF I WERE A SHARPENER

If I were a sharpener
I would go round.
I would sharpen your pencil.
You would watch the sharpenings
Going round.

I'd make your pencil snap.
I'd make it sharp and make it crack.

The sharpening starts to unwind
As you turn me round.
When you take me off, the sharpenings
Will drop.

Rhianna Briars (9)
Danemill CP School

I'D LIKE TO BE . . .

I'd like to be an artist,
I'd like to fly a plane,
I'd like to be a farmer,
I'd like to be a cook.

I'd like to be a superstar,
I'd like to be a pop star,
But just before I start,
I'd like to read a book.

Alana Brown (9)
Danemill CP School

THE FUNNY DRAGON

I know a great big dragon,
You may think this is funny,
But this great big dragon,
Is actually like a bunny.

He is very soft,
He has a fluffy tail,
He lives up in my loft,
His squawk is like a quail.

He has big floppy ears,
When we have leaks,
I think they're his tears,
The reason he cries
He doesn't like the creaks.

Sophie Tierney (9)
Danemill CP School

IF I WERE

If I were a footballer
Rushing past the crowd.
I'd visit Wembley
And pick up the crown.

If I were a basketball player
I would be six feet.
I'd jump very high.
To eat my apple pie.

Alexander McLoughlin (8)
Danemill CP School

ME AND MY FAMILY

Me and my family
Are always having fun
Going to the beach
Having a sticky bun.

Me and my family
Like going out
Going on walks
Running about.

Me and my family
Like to play games
Going to see people
Looking after the Great Danes.

Me and my family
Are always singing,
Dancing, playing and
Always praying.

Amy Barden (9)
Danemill CP School

FAIRY, FAIRY

Fairy, fairy where are you?
Fairy, fairy what do you do?
Fairy, fairy I like you.

Fairy, fairy how are you?
Fairy, fairy I can't see you,
Fairy, fairy why can't I?
Fairy, fairy what's your name?

Shelley Manley (8)
Danemill CP School

MY SISTER

She's lovely and nice and kind,
My sister is called Alice,
And she ought to live in a palace,
She can be a devil, but not much.

You'd better look out for Alice,
She takes your clothes and make-up,
And she goes to the pub with me.

I buy her a drink,
And get her some food,
To make her happy,
She's called Alice!

Rachel Walton (8)
Danemill CP School

MY PET DOG

My pet dog can bark
he is a silly lark
he rolls in mud
so he is a pud.

My pet dog is naughty
so he is forty
he runs around and around
so he falls to the ground.

Susan Ellis (9)
Danemill CP School

DOWN AT THE BOTTOM OF THE DEEP BLUE SEA

Down at the bottom of the deep blue sea,
There's a big, scary monster waiting for you and me,

I wouldn't go down there he might take a bite,
So if I was you I'd stay out of sight,

Some people say he is very scary,
But the others just say he's big and hairy,

I can't just stay here, I've got to find out,
What all this nonsense is all about!

So here I am down in my submarine,
All the seaweed is very nice and green.

So where is the monster? I forgot to bring my map,
If you see him give him a loud clap.

Then suddenly I saw him near a dark, gloomy cave,
I hope if he sees me I won't have to be his slave.

I walked over to him, he said 'Hello,
Please would you get me a cup of cocoa?'

Now I know what his behaviour is like,
It's so pleasant I could ride my bike.

Naomi Bedford (8)
Danemill CP School

SPACE

I was born in space,
with an unusal face.
When my mum saw me,
she desperately tried,
to get rid of me.

Samuel Putnam (8)
Danemill CP School

I AM IN SPACE

I am in space,
The orange, hot sun shining,
Too hot to go near,
The colours mixing yellow, red and orange.

I am in space,
All the planets orbiting,
Different colours,
Venus, Mars and many more.

I am in space,
The moon, very hot or very cold,
The craters, deep and wide,
It's really, really dry.

I am in space,
The Milky Way,
The galaxy,
The twinkling stars.

Michelle Richards (9)
Granby Primary School

SPACE MONSTER

Yesterday I saw an alien,
He was probably from outer space,
He must have been rather scary,
He frightened the whole human race!

He walked down the street,
And gave a person a fit,
He called a man a 'Dumbo,'
(He was a hypocrite!)

He ran into Woolworth's,
And purchased a PlayStation game,
Now he needed a credit card,
But nobody asked for his name.

He started to play with a Barbie,
Then he found some jelly and a candy cane,
He climbed into a BMW,
And drove in the complete wrong lane!

Today I saw his spaceship,
It was red, fat and tall,
Off he went back to his own planet,
From then on no one saw him at all.

Natalie Jade Ellis (9)
Granby Primary School

IN SPACE

I'm going into space
I've got to get my ace case
I want to see a Martian,
green and tall and scary too.
I think I can see a Martian now
I have to get my tea now.
So I will go to that shop.
I've got a flea from my tea.
Now I need a pea.
When I got back my tea was cold
So now on my holidays I'll go to the sun
'I'll get hot pud that's for sure,' said the little girl.
Then the little girl went home and took her case home too.
In the case was the Martian
So watch out because the Martian is about.

Jenna Whitehead (10)
Granby Primary School

THE VAMPIRE

I know it's there, under the stair
Waiting to pounce, waiting to bounce
So should I take a look?

I'm talking about a vampire, that I heard a long time ago
So shall I be brave and open that door?

Now come on Graham, go down and open the door
So I opened the door . . .
'*Boo!* Hi I'm so sorry got to go. Sorry I didn't say hello.'

Graham Pickering (10)
Granby Primary School

SPACE

Space is ace,
Is there a second kind of race?
Do they have an ugly face?
Are they as thin as lace?

Do they live on Mars?
Or do they live in jars?
Do they drive cars
To get around the stars?

Do they eat meat?
Or do they chew feet?
That would be neat,
If that is all they eat.

Paul Martin (9)
Granby Primary School

I'VE ALWAYS WONDERED

I've always wondered if the Sun could cook a ginormous bun.
I've always wondered if Mercury was so hot it couldn't be.
I've always wondered if Venus would ever lead us.
I've always wondered about Earth and the answers to its birth.
I've always wondered if Mars got its colour from guitars.
I've always wondered if Jupiter went so fast it was like a cheetah.
I've always wondered if Saturn was made up of a pattern.
I've always wondered if Uranus had a turn to beat the trainers.
I've always wondered if Neptune had a lunch break dead on noon.
I've always wondered if Pluto would get a chance to grow and grow.
I've always wondered if the Moons could be eaten with giant spoons.

Carter-Nathaniel Green (11)
Granby Primary School

SPACE

Two little aliens from Pluto set off for the sun,
for their food supplies they took a large iced bun.
Flying through space in their super ship,
their instrument panel going *blip, blip, blip.*
They quickly passed Charon, Pluto's moon
and soon zoomed by blue Neptune.
Uranus came next, rolling on its side like a wheel.
As it got hotter their purple skin started to peel.
They went to Saturn, it's beautiful rings made of stone.
Mummy alien rang them from home.
Passing Jupiter with its great red spot
it was getting hotter than hot.
As they got nearer to Mars with its rusty-red colour
they ate a bit of their bun to make them fuller.
When the green, blue and brown of Earth was in sight
as they turned they nearly crashed into a satellite.
As they passed Venus they overtook a friend.
Their long journey was coming to an end.
They reached Mercury - no time for a rest -
it was too hot, they decided Pluto was best.
They turned around and zoomed back home
and phoned Mum on the telephone.

Hannah Solanki (9)
Granby Primary School

ON THE MOON

I walk slowly on the moon.
It's very, very quiet
there's green aliens everywhere.
I don't dare talk to them.

In case they might bite off my head
or eat me.
I feel I have been followed,
because they are behind me.

What shall I do?
The aliens have got four eyes
and ten arms.
They were green and slimy
I'm getting really, really hot.

I want to take my helmet off
but then I would die.
Do I want to die,
or do I want to be baking hot?

Why did I come on my own?

Nicole Pickett (10)
Granby Primary School

MY ALIEN FRIEND

My alien friend lives underneath my bed
She eats there, she sleeps there underneath the bed,
At night I creep out of bed to play with her
She gets out all my toys and makes me play with them
Then she makes me chase her around the house,
She makes me roll over and hide under the sofa.

Then she jumps in the fish tank, but the fish don't mind,
My alien friend is a green and orange blob with two arms and legs
She loves to eat chocolate, *yummy, yummy, yum.*
She hates to eat curry, *yuk, yuk, yuk.*
Her favourite game is hide and seek
She hides in the most unusual places
All in the middle of the night.

Rebecca Gisborne (10)
Granby Primary School

MY WITCH

I had a witch called Winnie
She had long, green hair
And purple eyes
And wore a bright pink pinny!

I had a witch called Winnie
She used to boil frogs
And lizards with long legs,
She'd eat them for her dinner,
And serve them up with pegs!

I had a witch called Winnie
She'd love to play a game.
It didn't matter,
Win or lose,
She enjoyed it all the same!

I had a witch called Winnie
A nice witch, happy and playful
Although the things she did were strange,
She made my life delightful.

Harriet Newcombe (10)
Granby Primary School

THE FIRST MAN ON THE MOON

Neil Armstrong was the first man on the moon
The news got round very soon.
'The eagle has landed,' is what he said.
The two men he led
One small step for man
One giant leap for mankind
They bounced on the moon,
With not at all any gloom.
They had lost all their sorrow to be filled with joy
Like a kid with a new toy.
They were famous to all
When they got back they had a ball
And still are famous to all.

Emma Smith (11)
Granby Primary School

PLANETS

Planets are red
Planets are blue
Planets are yellow
And so are you.
If planets are red
If planets are blue
If planets are yellow
How could it be true?
Everyone knows that they're blue!

Garreth Goodwin (11)
Granby Primary School

A BEAUTIFUL MOSQUE

A mosque is where Muslims pray to God,
And when it's Eid, they say, 'Eid Mubark' in a surprised way.
When men shake people's hands.
Do you know why other people shake other people's hands,
It's because they want to greet other people. That's why!

Anisah Khalifah (8)
Highfields Primary School

ALL ABOUT THE SEA

I like the sea because,
of the noise it makes
it makes quiet sounds
which I like because
it sounds like the wind blowing the sea
and the fish swimming slowly.
The sea's moods are sometimes angry
and sometimes calm but still the fish swim slowly.

Muhammad Abdullatif (8)
Highfields Primary School

MY POEM

I wish I could fly to Saudi Arabia
Because my mum is going to Saudi Arabia
And I'm going to miss her
I'm going to stay with my grandmother
But I'm really going to miss her.

Mariam Sayani (7)
Highfields Primary School

MY CAT

I wish I had a cat because it has fur.
I can cuddle it and I like the sharp nails.
I can feed it with milk and meat
And I like the long tail
And I like the eyes in the dark
And I like the whiskers and the paws.
I would like to take it for a walk and play with it.

Irum Igbal (8)
Highfields Primary School

MY DOG

I love my dog because he has a long tail,
I love my dog because he is a black Labrador cross,
I love my dog because he plays with my cat,
I love my dog because he can open doors by himself,
I love my dog because his name is Duke,
I miss my dog because he went to the farm to help the farmer.

Christopher Bramley (9)
Highfields Primary School

MY KITTEN

I wish I had a kitten so I could take it for a walk,
The kitten would have his own basket to sleep in.
I would give the kitten his own milk at night.
The kitten would be spiky.
The kitten would go to sleep at 9.15.
I like kittens because they are small and quiet.

Sumaiya Ismail (7)
Highfields Primary School

TELETUBBIES

Jelly babies, jelly babies
Like Teletubbies,
Teletubbies, Teletubbies, like
Jelly babies, jelly babies,
Po likes red jelly,
Laa-Laa likes yellow jelly
Dipsy likes green jelly
Tinky Winky likes purple jelly,
Noo Noo likes blue jelly.

Nadia Gaffar (7)
Highfields Primary School

MY NASTY SPELL

A very nasty spell it is,
To make the cauldron pop and fizz
This isn't a very funny joke
In fact it's serious to make you choke.
Put your finger in the bowl,
Then put in a dried, dead mole.
Not a flower, not a cake,
But a slimy poisonous snake.
If you get a sneezing cold,
You will soon get very old.
Some silky hair
We do not care
You have sung the song
So you have got the pong.
A very nasty spell it is
To make the cauldron pop and fizz.

Rosie Johnson (9)
Little Hill Primary School

MUM

My mum
Cuddles me
Cleans me
Feeds me
And plays with me.

She also hits me
Organises me
Tidies me
And teases me.

She tries to
Homework me
Trust me
Library me
And please me.

But best of all she
Tickles me
Easter eggs me
Pocket moneys me
And simply thinks the world of me.

Daniel Fragnoli (8)
Little Hill Primary School

FROST

Frost is slippery, silvery and spiky
It's white and has no colour,
Biting frost in the morning winds,
A crisp, cold and crunchy day ahead.

Ruth Harbord (8)
Little Hill Primary School

THIS IS THE BOY

This is the boy,
This is the boy who kicked the ball.
This is the boy who kicked the ball.
That hit the vase.

This is the vase,
This is the vase that smashed into pieces
When the ball hit it.

This is the mother,
This is the mother of the boy who kicked the ball,
That hit the vase and smashed it all.

This is the mother who shouted at the boy,
Who kicked the ball that hit the vase
And smashed it all.

Daniel Jones (8)
Little Hill Primary School

JUNGLE ANIMALS

In the jungle lions roar,
The hippopotamuses always snore.
The hyenas always chitter, chatter,
Mr Monkey is a mad hatter.
Snakes slide, slither and hiss,
And the elephants always miss a chance for a kiss.
Mrs Giraffe and her long, long neck,
The baby flamingo only gives a little peck,
And pandas will always be black and white.

Monica Mohindra (9)
Little Hill Primary School

BIRD'S EYE

I wish I could fly
Like a sparrow in the sky.

I wish I could soar
Like an eagle.

I wish I could dive
Like a seagull.

If only I had wings
I too would take
To the sky.

I fly using my
Bird's Eyes.

Christopher Mark (9)
Little Hill Primary School

NAUGHTY BOY

Naughty baby in his cot,
Trying to figure out his plot,
All he is, is a naughty boy,
Never bringing anyone joy,
Babysitter's coming round
Naughty boy doesn't make a sound
Because he's wiping on his cot
Stuff like bogies, stuff like snot
Babysitter puts him on his potty
But it goes on her lap and she goes dotty.

Sharon Rivers (9)
Little Hill Primary School

MUM

My mum
Combs me
Feeds me
Cleans me
Sometimes she tries to
Dry me
Eat me
Fry me
Sizzle me
My mum likes to
Cook me
Mend me
Anger me
But best of all she
Loves me.

Peter Sumpter (8)
Little Hill Primary School

MY FAMILY

My mummy she keeps with the beat
And she has smelly feet.
My daddy likes jelly
And has got a big belly.
My hamster is grey
And makes his bed out of hay.
My brother thinks he is cool
But I think he is a fool.

Lauren Dawkins (9)
Little Hill Primary School

BUBBLE, BUBBLE, TOIL AND TROUBLE

Bubble, bubble, sizzle and suzzle,
Cauldron burn and cauldron bubble,
Full of evil, full of trouble,
Bubble, bubble, sizzle and suzzle.

Bubble, bubble, make and bake,
I am going to put in
The scale of a snake,
And teeth of a rake,
Bubble, bubble, make and bake.

Bubble, bubble, toil and moil,
Inside this spell I'll put soil.

Witch Amanda
Witch Varander,
Chant this song
All day long.

Victoria Ritchie (9)
Little Hill Primary School

INSANE

Tony Blair turned into a hare,
Adam, well a lion had 'im,
My friend Ben turned into a hen,
My friend Mat turned into a bat,
My friend Gina turned into a hyena,
My friend Riahn, well she went to the museum,
Mr Fragnoly ate too much ravioli,
And Miss Va Voom went coboom
When she sat on the moon.

Leigh Cracknell (8)
Little Hill Primary School

HE THOUGHT HE SAW

He thought he saw an octopus,
That climbed up to his knee,
He looked again and found it was,
A nice hot cup of tea,
'A thing I remember,' he said,
'Is when I squashed a flea!'

He thought he saw a bumblebee,
That stung him on his head,
He looked again and found it was,
A little slice of bread,
'Unless I eat the bread,' he said
'My bee sting will have bled!'

He thought he saw a cute hamster,
That ran about his cage,
He looked again and found it was,
A massive plant of sage.
'It is not very good,' he said,
'Because I'm at old age!'

Louise Davis (9)
Little Hill Primary School

THIS IS THE GIRL

This is the girl
This is the girl who mushed a lollipop,
This is the girl who mushed a lollipop with a fork,
This is the girl who mushed a lollipop with a fork and broke the glass.
This is the father,
This is the father who never found out about the girl
Who mushed a lollipop with a fork and broke the glass.

Rachel Sim (8)
Little Hill Primary School

THE BROKEN VINEGAR

This is the boy.
This is the boy who dropped the vinegar.
This is the boy who dropped the vinegar
all over the floor.

This is the father.
This is the father of the boy who dropped
the vinegar
all over the floor.

This is the father who sent the boy
who dropped the vinegar
all over the floor
to bed!

Benjamin Irvine (8)
Little Hill Primary School

I LOVE MY MUM

My mum looks after me
In the morning she brightens up my day,
She pocket monies me, Easter eggs me,
And presents me.

She reads me, organises me,
Spellings me
My mum teaches me.

But best of all she
Cuddles me,
Kisses me,
And loves me.

Katherine Allen (8)
Little Hill Primary School

UNTITLED

Antelope's eat ants,
Bamboos bother bananas,
Cats can somersault through caterpillar hoops,
Dinosaurs dance all day long,
England annoys Egypt's king,
Funny frogs play fiddles,
Gina the giraffe growls like a lion,
Hippos hip hop and have fun,
Igloos annoy Eskimos,
Jack in the box,
Kate the kangaroo jumps all over the place,
Liam the lion loved Laura, Laura likes lamb,
Mark the monkey made marshmallows
Nathan needs Nelly his mum,
Olivia the octopus on an orange,
Peter Piper picked a peck of peppers,
Queens are quite, quite, quick,
Rachel the rectangular rabbit,
Sam the slithering snake on sand,
Tyler the tamed tiger,
Unicorns under umbrellas,
Victory for the vulture,
Walk away from washed whales,
X-rays, x-rays,
Yaks, yak up all over yoghurt,
Zebras' suits zip up.

Olivia Elton (8)
Little Hill Primary School

THE BIRDS AND I

I wish I could fly
Like an eagle in the sky

I wish I could drift
Just like a swift

I wish I could squawk
Just like a hawk

I wish I could soar
Like a jackdaw

I wish I could go like an arrow
Just like a sparrow

And if I was a thrush
I would rush

And if I were a crow
I'd go very, very slow
You know!

Michael Woodford (9)
Little Hill Primary School

THE BOY WHO KICKED THE BALL

This is the boy.
This is the boy who kicked the ball.
This is the boy who kicked the ball in the room.
This is the boy who kicked the ball in the room, breaking the toy.
This is the mum who didn't know about the boy
Who kicked the ball in the room, breaking the toy.

Jamie Broughton (8)
Little Hill Primary School

MUM

My mum
Helps me
Cuddles me
Reads me
Sleeps me
She loves me
Pocket moneys me
Teases me
She trusts me
Easter Eggs me
Cleans me
And feeds me
But best of all is when Mum
Birthday presents me
Tickles me
Surprises me
And tidies me.

Sam Birchall (8)
Little Hill Primary School

TWINKLE, TWINKLE

Twinkle, twinkle little bat,
How I wonder what you're at,
Up above the world so high,
Like a teacher in the sky,
Twinkle, twinkle little bat,
How I wonder what you're at.

Hannah Usher (8)
Little Hill Primary School

I Put In The Pot

One, two, three I put in the pot,
One too many what a lot,
A pair of feet, an eye of frog,
A blade of grass, a piece of fog,
Toe of cow, and wool of sheep,
Head of baby, crying and weep,
Snake's long neck, a bluebird's wing,
A cat's sharp claw, a hand of a king
One, two, three I put in the pot,
One too many what a lot.

Sara Bentley (9)
Little Hill Primary School

The Cauldron

Vampire's blood and its own old teeth,
Cauldron bubble, double the trouble,
Twenty four frogs' legs, eye of a bat,
Cauldron bubble, double the trouble.
Crocodile's tail, crocodile's froth,
Cauldron bubble, double the trouble.
Tip of a dog's tongue, tip of its toe
Cauldron bubble, double the trouble.

Sophie Porter (9)
Little Hill Primary School

THE SPELL

Get the blood of a vampire bat,
Get the tail of a big black rat,
Throw it in the big cauldron,
And get a big and smelly thumb,
Get the sheet with my smelly list,
Let's see a big smelly fist.
Kill the people in the city,
It really is a big pity.

Michael Mark (9)
Little Hill Primary School

I KNOW A BEE

I know a bee that flew to Japan and stung a man!
I know a bee that landed in a pan!
I know a bee that got stuck in a can!
I know a bee that had a tan!
I know a bee that hit a man!
I know a bee that did the can-can dance!
I know a bee that ate some All Bran!
I know a bee who's called Dan!

Daniel Brown (9)
Little Hill Primary School

TOFFEE

Toffee is sticky
Toffee is nice and yummy
Toffee is yummy.

Carly Evans (9)
Little Hill Primary School

A WICKED POTION

An eye of a newt and foot of a bat,
Scale of a dragon and tongue of a cat,
What else can I find?
What else will I need
To give my cauldron a little feed!
All of these things go inside in slow motion
To make my wicked witch's potion.

Nicola Eassom (9)
Little Hill Primary School

MY LUCKY TREE

My lucky tree is gold,
My lucky tree has flowers,
My lucky tree is always there for me,
My lucky tree can talk,
My lucky tree can write,
My lucky tree is always lucky.

Sonam Sood (9)
Little Hill Primary School

BEST FRIENDS

Best friends we'll always be,
Sally, Esme, Natasha and me,
We talk, laugh and always play,
So we're best friends at the end of the day.

Adele Rolston-Bates (9)
Little Hill Primary School

FOOTBALL PITCH

F lying ball up in the sky,
O nside attacker just scored a goal,
O ffside winger that's a shame,
T. ime to blow the full-time whistle,
B all on the penalty spot,
A dvantage said the referee,
L ast round of the FA Cup,
L eft winger running down the wing,

P layer goes down in the area,
I t could be a booking,
T ottenham lose the final to Man U,
C elebration time,
H alf-time whistle goes.

Ben Hall (8)
Little Hill Primary School

THE SMELLY SPELL

Blood of a vampire bat with frog's toes,
In the black cauldron, quick in it goes,
Scales of dragons, tongue of an adder,
Snake's slime and a human bladder,
Lots of newts and a lizard's tail,
Get lots of rats and big gutsy wail,
Then get toads and lots of slimy snakes,
Then the black cauldron bakes, bakes, bakes.

James Gardner (9)
Little Hill Primary School

SPORT

I like playing sport
My best is football,
But all the footballers are too tall.
My second best sport is cricket,
When my friend only flicks it
I really hit it.
My third is blading,
When my wheels are failing.
My fourth is snooker,
But I hit the ball like a bazooka.
My fifth is rugby,
But people try to hug me.

Scott Daniel Dalby (9)
Little Hill Primary School

JACK FROST

On the ground lies the glittering frost where Jack Frost put it,
There it lies all white and slippery.
I ran my foot over a patch of ice.
I thought it was rock hard.
How it was glistening in daylight. It was freezing.
The frost was wet and drippy, shimmery, spiky and silvery,
The frost was crunchy, crispy and cold.
On the ground lies the frost.
It was cold as the North Pole.

Melisa Kostrzewski (8)
Little Hill Primary School

SPORT FOREVER

Football, tennis whatever you like,
Have a game whenever you like,
Sport is great,
Wonderful to play,
Take your pick,
And play it your way, however you like,
Meet your opponent,
Beat your opponent.

Play it cool and don't be a fool,
Play the game it's really cool,
On the ice, under the sea
It's really cool just follow me.
Racing on your feet,
Racing on a horse,
Racing all around and running on the course.

Motor racing is your friend,
Watch the cars come round the bend,
We want all the games to start,
Using our electric go-kart
Round and round the little bend
We want everyone to be your friend.

Enter the race and try to get first place
We want you to go and win,
So don't throw your chance in the bin,
We all know sport is great, don't we!

Daniel Nogher (8)
Little Hill Primary School

MY ALIEN

Great big creature
Under Mars and near Jupiter
Munching away at Mercury
Dropping rock dust everywhere
Riding on a scrap moon buggy
Probably coming this way.

Anthony Meads (8)
Little Hill Primary School

I DO NOT LIKE MY DOCTOR

I do not like thee Doctor Fell,
The reason why I cannot tell,
But thee I know full well,
I do not like thee Doctor Fell.

Elisha Sally Lee (8)
Little Hill Primary School

LYN AND THE PIN

There once was a lady called Lyn,
Who had a very thin pin,
The lady grew fat,
And the pin broke her back,
So that was the end of Lyn.

Hayley Slatford (8)
Little Hill Primary School

THE SUNNY PICNIC

We're having a picnic, it's very sunny,
I must eat my sandwiches but they're not very yummy.
(I think it might be because they're made by Mummy)
Mum heard that and said, 'That's not very funny!'

I went on the swing, and I felt I was going to sing,
I went so high, I saw a netballer on the left wing,
I heard something and it was my mum calling me in.

Yeliz Sönmez & Katie Collins (9)
Little Hill Primary School

SAM THE SNAIL

Sam the snail slithers
Silently through
The trees and rocks.

Lee Corrigan (9)
Little Hill Primary School

THE WITCH'S CAULDRON

Boil, boil, bubble, bubble,
In the cauldron goes the trouble.
An eye of a bat and the tail of a cat,
Then in goes a mouldy rat,
Two eyes from a snake,
In my cauldron boil, boil, bubble and bake.

Emma Jane Ince (9)
Little Hill Primary School

DIFFERENT SEASONS

Snow, snow winter snow
Slow to come
And quick to go.

Snow, snow winter snow
Slippery, slidey,
Skiddy and sparkly.

Spring, spring, summer, spring
Bring the world to see
Spring, spring, summer, spring
Bring your friends to tea.

Spring, spring, summer, spring
Flowers that grow,
And birds that sing
Oh look at the joy they bring.

Rain, rain autumn rain
Run to school and
Back again.

Rain, rain, autumn rain
Leaves are blowing
Down the lane.

Emma Stenfalt (9)
Little Hill Primary School

THE EVIL EYE

There once was an evil eye,
Who had to say goodbye.

His potion was weird,
It contained a black beard.
It had the eye of a cat,
A big fat rat,
A mouse with a shoe,
An owl that went *whoo*
A horrible witch,
With a big itch.

There once was an evil eye,
Who had to say goodbye.

Daniel Haslum (8)
Little Hill Primary School

RAP

There once was a creature from outer space,
Who had a really weird face,
He got a place in a race,
But blew it because he knew he couldn't do it,
So next time you see a creature from outer space
Don't give him a race.

Carly Wright (8)
Little Hill Primary School

DOUBLE DOUBLE TOIL AND TROUBLE

Double, double, toil and trouble
Try and bake a cake
Sing a song and don't be long
Boil and bake a great big steak
With a smelly sock and a smelly big dog
River flowing like bubbles are glowing
Get some gum and spoil some fun.

Double, double, toil and trouble.

Taran Uppal (8)
Little Hill Primary School

WILD WIND'S WHISTLE

Wild wind, wild wind, swirl, swirl
It stops once or twice, three or four.
It kicks the sink and hurts its swirl.
It beats at the window all day long
It hurts the door.
It takes the goal.
Wild wind, wild wind, swirl, swirl,
Don't stop.

Rasheed Ismail (8)
Little Hill Primary School

DOUBLE, DOUBLE TOIL AND TROUBLE

Double, double toil and trouble,
Try and bake a cake
Sing a song and don't be long,
Boil and bake a great big steak
A smelly sock and a big, big dog.

River flowing like bubble glowing
Get some gum and spoil some fun.

Double, double toil and trouble.

Charlotte Ann Starmer (9)
Little Hill Primary School

LOVEABLE TROUBLE

Kissy, kissy, burn a bubble,
Make it so it's double trouble.

Whizzy, whizzy let's get busy,
Break a heart and have some fizzy pop,
Then you will end up being very slow
Then put in a touch of snow,
A tail or a rat to make a bat,
Kissy, kissy, burn a bubble,
Make it so it's double trouble.

Natalie Sara Khan (9)
Little Hill Primary School

SUMMER POEM

Summer is here
Umbrellas are waiting for a rainy day
Mothers are cheerful
My sister is as happy as happy as can be
Ears are hot
Roses are blooming

People are happy
On the other side of the world it is winter
Explorers are boiling hot
Mouths want water.

Selina Boullin (9)
Medway Community Primary School

WINTER POEM

W ind swishing through the trees
I   ce all slippery.
N   ight coming early.
T   rees covered with snow.
E   ars all frozen and pink.
R   udolph's nose is bright red.

P   eople are frozen.
O   utside snow is falling.
E   ars all stiff and frozen.
M outh chattering.

Zainab Lorgat (9)
Medway Community Primary School

GOOSEBUMPS EVERYWHERE

I look at Goosebumps before I read and realise
it's very hard to breathe.
I look at the cover and then discover how
hard they are to read.
I try my best like it's a test but then the book's
getting scary.
Until I hear the name Mary
'Mary' yells a boy, 'I've lost my toy.'
Huh! Now it's getting scary!
I look in the mirror 'Ahh, it's a bad hair day.'
Oh, phew, I realise I don't have to pay.
'You can't scare me,' says the wolf of Fever Swamp.
Now it's getting more scary, I think I need a chomp.
'Ow!' That's what I scream.
Then I wake up realising it's just a dream.
I get up in a shock and hear the cuckoo clock
Cuckoo! Cuckoo!
Cuckoo clock of what? Cuckoo clock of doom.
Now I'm running in a boom to my mum's room.

Ramiah O'Neill
Medway Community Primary School

SPOOKY

S keletons dancing
P eople cracking
O *ooh* say ghosts
O ld people changing into ghosts
K icking skeletons
Y ou crossing the line of death.

Mohammed Sacranie (10)
Medway Community Primary School

GOOSEBUMPS WONDER

When I look at Goosebumps it says, 'Try it if you dare.'
I don't know if I should try it, it might give me a stare,
Or when I read the titles like it said 'The haunted Mask'
I don't know if it will jump at me or do a scary cast
When I am trying to run away in a girl's bikini
When it's backing up on me I'm wishing for a genie
'Cause I didn't like the genie I stuffed him in the mud
After that I felt quite pleased with myself . . .
                I thought I had done really good.

Dean Grant (9)
Medway Community Primary School

EID MUBARAK

Eid is green because the flag is green
Eid is having fun at the fair
Imam calls us to pray
My dad buys the Eid clothes
My mother cooks ready for Eid
My brother going to the mosque
My auntie's coming to my house ready for fun.
After we go to a friend's house.
The kitchen needs cleaning.

Nasema Akthar (9)
Medway Community Primary School

STREET BALL

Eugine gets the ball and runs top speed to the hoop
Runs one mile and the crowd goes wild
He tries to pass to a partner but the partner misses it
It hits the rails and goes 'Thunk'
Somebody gets it and starts to fly.
The other team cry as he goes for a slam . . .

Dunk!

Ngaturue Jackman (9)
Medway Community Primary School

EID

Eid is the colour green,
Eid tastes sweet and lovely,
The smell tastes like chocolate barfi.
On Eid I go to people's houses,
Imam calls you to pray,
I am happy on Eid day.

Alisha Datt (9)
Medway Community Primary School

WINTER

W   inter is cold.
I   ce falling down.
N   oise is coming from outside.
T   he rain is falling like water.
E   vening is cold like a freezer.
R   ain is coming down from the sky.

Shenaz Choudory (9)
Medway Community Primary School

CHICKEN

It's a feathered bird,
that goes 'Cluck, cluck,'
it lives on the farm
and sometimes hangs around with the ducks,
it lays eggs, sometimes one, sometimes
several, sometimes white, sometimes brown,
and I have an egg for breakfast
on my toast round.

Sophia Patel (9)
Medway Community Primary School

EID MUBARUK

Eid is happiness.
Imam calls to pray.
Dates are eaten by those who fast.
Mum makes very good food.
Uncles come to eat in my house with joy.
Brothers go to pray (Namaz)
Aunties and mums cook in the kitchen.
Rings and clothes people wear.
Upstairs people will be dressing up.
Kinds of presents people will receive.

Mohammed Ahsanul Hoque
Medway Community Primary School

DIANA

D iana was a loving helpful person.
I n some countries she visited sick people
A nd I liked Diana because she was caring.
N ext morning my mum started to cry
A nd I wanted to cry too.

Rohini Sirichand (8)
Mellor Primary School

RESPECT

R espect other cultures.
E ven your family.
S how respect to other visitors in school.
P erhaps I shall play with everyone.
E veryone will be kind to you.
C an you respect other children?
T ake care of school property.

Gnayeta Samani (8)
Mellor Primary School

WINTER

W inter is fun.
I like winter.
N ext day I had a snowball fight.
T hat's when I was happy.
E very day when it snows in winter I
R ace downstairs and play with my sister.

Mayur Mistry (9)
Mellor Primary School

RESPECT

R espect old people
E verybody needs help
S ome people need friends
P eople need help
E verybody needs care
C are for everybody
T ake care.

Andrew Skeemer (8)
Mellor Primary School

RESPECT

R espect your family.
E ven respect others.
S ave people when they need help.
P eople should be nice to other people.
E verybody should be kind to other people.
C are for other people.
T ake care of others and your family.

Hetal Pala (8)
Mellor Primary School

WINTER

W inter, winter,
I s so cold,
N aming lots of things about winter is dreary,
T aking stuff in winter is bad.
E njoy winter and snow.
R ace downstairs and play with snow.

Jiten Anand (8)
Mellor Primary School

GOOD CHARACTER

Being humble, not boastful.
Fulfilling a promise or a trust.
Because in the end honesty is best.
Showing kindness to others because everyone
loves people who care for others, like lending
a helpful hand to someone in need because
'a friend in need is a friend indeed'.
Being forgiving when in power.
Having good thoughts about others.
Giving good advice when asked.
Ignoring matters that don't concern you.
Being patient and happy with what you've got.
Keeping a secret a secret.
Asking for forgiveness when at fault.

These are some of the things that lead to a happier life.

Fatima Hussein (9)
Mellor Primary School

DIANA

D iana was helpful.
I   liked her because she was loving,
A nd she was amazing. We all
N eed her.
A nd she was brave.

Afra Osman (8)
Mellor Primary School

WINTER

W inter is frosty and icy.
I ce is skiddy and slippy.
N oses get cold in winter.
T oes are cold when you go outside.
E veryone hopes there is snow.
R ain comes with snow and it is all slushy.

Veekash & Kisan Umrania (9)
Mellor Primary School

DIANA

D iana was helpful.
I was about to cry when I heard Diana had died.
A nyone who had illness, she cared for them.
N ow I'm sad because our Princess has died,
A nd she was very kind.

Neha Karia (9)
Mellor Primary School

WINTER

W inter, windy, wet weather,
I cy, slippery road,
N othing but snow,
T ravelling to school on a cold day,
E very day it gets colder,
R aining and cold all day.

Priten Thakrar (8)
Mellor Primary School

SEASON POEM

Oh, spring is coming,
What beautiful flowers,
Oh, summer's coming,
We have lots of fun,
We shall go to the seaside,
It will be hot,
Oh, autumn's coming,
We are going to see coloured leaves,
Oh, winter's coming,
We'll have lots of fun,
Playing in the snow,
Making snowmen.

Vandana Lad (8)
Mellor Primary School

THE CAT, DOG AND SPRING

The cat saw the milk
The dog saw the cat
The cat saw the dog
The cat ran
The dog ran after
The mouse drank the milk
Spring comes
Plants grow
Summer comes
The sun shines
Plants flower,
Autumn comes,
Leaves fall.

Tejasvi Sankada (8)
Mellor Primary School

WINTER

W inter is wonderful, winter is exciting,
I cicles are dripping like rain,
N ow it's time for the snow to fall,
T iny flakes of snow start falling,
E arly morning snow stops falling.
R ain starts falling, oh dear!

Sona Nathwani (9)
Mellor Primary School

WINTER

W hen it is winter the nights get dark.
I t is icy in winter.
N ow is the time to play with snow.
T omorrow it's going to snow!
E at lovely yummy yummy food.
R ain, rain, please stop!

Bhakti Makwana (8)
Mellor Primary School

WINTER

W hen winter winds are cold and breezy
I cicles are hanging from the roof's edge,
N o leaves are on the trees,
T issue-like snow is falling outside,
E very day seems cold and colder, and,
R unning in the snow is very great fun.

Daniel Stewart-Dexter (9)
Mellor Primary School

I WENT TO THE ZOO

I went to the zoo,
I went to the crocodile,
It went *'Snap! Snap!'*
Next I went to the tiger,
It went *'Rrrah! Rrrah!'*
Next I went to the snakes
They went *'Sssssss!'*
Next I went to the cocks
They went *'Cock a doodle doo!'*
Next I went to the mice
They went *'Squeak! Squeak!'*
Next I went home, *'Phew!'*

Sonam Chaggar (8)
Mellor Primary School

WINTER

W inter is slippery and it is cold,
I n winter it is dark and you can't see anything,
N obody can see the slippery slopes,
T ravelling on a snowy day,
E veryone is happy,
R ight, I'm going out to make a snowman.

Nabeel Boliya (8)
Mellor Primary School

POEM

The stars are big
But from far away they look very small
Sometimes they are bigger than the sun
The stars are bright
And wonderful.

Chirag V Limbachia (9)
Mellor Primary School

A COSMIC POEM

Space! Space!
A great big chase,
Planets big and planets small,
Astronauts only one foot tall.

Spaceman, rockets,
A suit with pockets,
Bye, bye, to my home,
Steady on, watch out for that cone.

'Ah! A Martian, turn back quick,
Give that lever a good old kick,'
'No, no, you silly fool,
He needs some help to keep his cool.'

'No, no, please stop,
He's gonna blow his mean green top!'
Back to Earth with a great, big thud.
We landed in a lot of mud.

Kyla Archer (9)
Millfield Primary School

UP THERE IN SPACE

Once I shot up into space
In this really weird case.
I landed on a yellow round ball.
It really seemed to be quite small.

Then this snotty green creature
Came along and asked if he had a feature.
I said 'No.'
He said 'Oh so!'

But then I decided to travel along.
You'll never guess what I saw.
Some people playing ping-pong.

Then I went back and said
'I wish I landed in my bed.'
Now I see the planet Mars
Pictured in the yellow stars.

Claire Graham (9)
Millfield Primary School

SPACEMAN

There once was a man
That lived in outer space
He travelled around
In a little suitcase.

He's very mean,
He's purple and green
He's red and yellow
Blue and cream.

Joseph Byland (9)
Millfield Primary School

COSMIC WORLD

I woke up, I found myself in space,
I saw some aliens pacing towards me, pace by pace.
They were dark green, some scarlet red.
Still I wish I was in my bed.

They took me to their spaceship and offered me a drink,
I drank a bit, it made me sick, I desperately ran to the sink.
Their drink was yellow, their food was pink,
Then turned all lumpy, then turned to ink.

Their back garden was gloomy and dark,
There are a lot of spaceships, why don't they have a space park?
They have a weird creature for a pet, and it is purple.
Why can't they have simple pets, like a gerbil?

Sarah Naish (9)
Millfield Primary School

THE ALIEN

I went to space with my dad
I saw an alien that was really mad
He had red eyes with black in the middle
He really had a treat on the fiddle
He had a face, yellow and green
He really did look nasty and mean
He took us both up to Mars
We both saw a load of cars
It was really dark up there
So I was really scared.

Natalie Carr (9)
Millfield Primary School

WEIRD AND WONDERFUL SPACE

Rocket space,
It's a very big place,
Because it's a ride,
Who knows where they'll glide?
It's a race to get into space,
Meet a face,
It's a big disgrace!

I travelled to Mars,
And met lots of stars,
Maroon spacemen,
With a weird pen,
Planets are horrible green,
They don't look very clean.

I remember when I went to the moon,
First I heard a really big *zoom!*

Anoushka Kansara (9)
Millfield Primary School

ALIENS EVERYWHERE

Aliens, aliens, everywhere,
Shall I see them? Do you dare?
Some are red, some are green.
Some are kind, some are mean.
All of the aliens make different sounds
'Bleep, bleep, squeak, squeak!'
Some of them are quite weak.
Aliens, aliens, can change forms
Thin, fat, big or small.

Dionne Lawrence (9)
Millfield Primary School

COSMIC

Aliens all in a jam,
In space on the Milky Way.
All dirty black thick hay,
The aliens see light yellow stars.
Mercury, Venus, Earth and Mars,
All different alien cars.

Some are red and some are yellow,
On the sun and on the moon.
There is a really big room,
Where they have a lot of fun,
Especially when Jupiter is even loopier.

New aliens come.
The most especially best is ET,
He has three fingers and four eyes,
But his favourite food is *shepherds' pies!*

Fiona Brakes (9)
Millfield Primary School

IF I WERE . . .

If I were a bird,
I'd soar sky-high,
If I were a butterfly,
I'd fly till the night was nigh.
If I were a pheasant, I'd,
watch out for poachers.
But I know I'm me,
and I wouldn't like to be,
anyone but me!

Kate Conaron (9)
Old Mill Primary School

74

IF I . . .

If I were the sea
I'd toss and turn
and swallow up all the boats
that float around
on the deep blue sea.

I'd offer homes to creatures
and we'd all live happily ever after
down, down, down below the
        ocean of dreams . . .

Then glisten from the light
of the new horizon.

Rachael Knappier (8)
Old Mill Primary School

IF I . . .

If I were a snake,
I'd slither through a deep
dark forest!
Then poison a rat with
my deadly teeth!

I'd camouflage myself in
bright green grass.
Then I'd climb a very tall
cactus with *deadly sharp spikes!*

Arron Mee (8)
Old Mill Primary School

SNOWFLAKES

Snowflakes,
Snowflakes,

Falling on the ground,
Soft and white, furry and round,

Snowflakes,
Snowflakes,

On the ground,
Children making snowmen
All around.

Snowflakes,
Snowflakes,

Melted by the sun,
Children are singing
In the sun.

Victoria Lucas (9)
Old Mill Primary School

IF I WERE . . .

If I were summer I'd shine with all my might.
I'd make the flowers share their colours.
Then I'd play with the lambs and listen
to the sheep bleat.
I'd make the world a happy place.
Then I'd make it a very friendly world.
Then after that I'd shine with all my
glittery rays on a pond.
That's what I'd do if I were summer!

Phoebe Blockley Campton (9)
Old Mill Primary School

IF I WERE . . .

If I were a gibbon
I'd swing to each and
every tree, then I'd zoom
through the grass trying
to look for something
to eat.

Sam Lee (7)
Old Mill Primary School

IF . . .

If I were a star
I'd shine till dawn.
Then I'd glow brightly.
I'd be up in the sky
Shining so brightly
And then I'd go out
When the world woke up.

Michaela Gibbins (8)
Old Mill Primary School

IF . . .

If I were a storm
I'd make all the windows creak
then I'd rage through the sky.
I'd strike thunder all over the world,
and then roar a terrible *roar!*

Natalie Harris (8)
Old Mill Primary School

IF

If I were the sun I'd make everyone happy
then I'd swoop across the sky.
Then I'd burn the country out
and then I'd shine and shine
until I'm tired.

Lucy Bass (7)
Old Mill Primary School

IF

If I were the sun,
I'd roar in the sky.
Then I'd make you come out and play.
I'd laugh and play with you
And then go to the other side of the world.

Michael Milner (9)
Old Mill Primary School

IF

If I was the sea
I would twist and turn
and jump all over the place
and then I would catch a ride
and slide and I would say
'Let the tide come in so we
have lots of water so people
can swim there.'

Nathan Underhill (8)
Old Mill Primary School

WHAT IS . . . LOVE?

Love is a deep friendship
Sent from above in Heaven.
It is a warm, soft
beautiful feeling.
It can't be spoken
but can be found.
It is shared between two
people who don't say a sound.

That's Love!

Emma Marfleet (8)
Old Mill Primary School

IF

If I was the sea
I would toss boats up and down.
It would be hot, warm or cold.
I'd look after the fish,
they would live happily,
and the waves would be splashing
about all day long.
That's what I would do if
I was the sea.

Shaun Parsons (8)
Old Mill Primary School

IF . . .

If I were a dolphin
I'd swim to a hot country.
I'd dive deep and far.
I'd love every animal.
I'd swoop down to the creatures.
I'd jump to the moon.
I'd swim to Africa.

Jonathan Taylor (9)
Old Mill Primary School

IF

If I were the . . . storm
I'd go and rattle the windows
then I would go all pale.
I'd strike the world with thunder
and then I'd laugh and laugh.

Sharon Scarborough (9)
Old Mill Primary School

IF

If I was a dolphin
I would swim free
I would jump out of the water
If I were a dolphin
I would slide away from danger
And then I would fly away
In the sea.

Joe Needham (9)
Old Mill Primary School

IF

If I were a dragon I'd roar with
smoke coming out of my nose
and I would burn houses down.

I would live under a tree and eat
juicy children for supper and blow fire
out of my mouth.

Anne-Marie Adamson (7)
Old Mill Primary School

IF

If I was a bird
I would fly in the sky
And land on a tree
And then I would sing.

Ellie George Preson (7)
Old Mill Primary School

HYENAS

When hyenas have the giggles,
They will laugh all day long,
Then they begin to chuckle,
To giggle, to grin, to smile, to titter,
To jeer, to sneer, to snigger,
That's what hyenas do when they giggle.

Charlie Patel (9)
Overdale Junior School

I'M WET THROUGH

The water
  splashes all over my face,
  like spray over a ship at sea.

The water
  makes my feet cold and frozen,
  like ice cubes in a drift.

I wish I were dry,
I wish I were dry,
warm and cosy by the fire.

Pawan Sharma (8)
Overdale Junior School

A BIRD

A bird is furry, a bird is soft.
It likes to sing lots and lots.
It cheeps in winter,
Cheeps in autumn and even summer and spring.
It's like a never ending song.
The food it likes for its tea,
One monkey nut and sunflower seeds.
It sleeps in the night without a sound
Nice and quiet in town
But in the morning it wakes us all with its song.

Jaskiren Loyal (8)
Overdale Junior School

I'm Wet Through

The water
>whistles in my ear,
>as it whacks me in the face.

The water
>looks like see-through plastic
>as it twinkles in the sun.

The water
>feels like silk
>as you let your hand drag
>through the surface.

I love the rain,
I love the rain,
I can't wait
until it comes again.

Rosie Henderson (9)
Overdale Junior School

Summer's Day

On a summer's day children go to the park to play.
On a summer's day people drink cool drinks and eat ice-cream.
On a summer's day families go for a day out.
On a summer's day people have cool showers.
On a summer's day shorts and T-shirts are mostly worn.
On a summer's day some people cool off with a fan.
On a summer's day some people would feel tired.
On a summer's day I like
>Going to the beach!

Nikesh Patel (9)
Overdale Junior School

I'm Wet Through

The water
        splashes over my face
        like a dog shaking too close to me.

The water
        drips into my eyes
        like someone else's tears.

The water
        trickles through my hair
        like streams down a mountain.

I'm really soaked!
I'm really soaked!
But my mum thinks it's a big joke!

James Burnage (8)
Overdale Junior School

Please Be Quiet In Room Nine

I like talking, I never stop.
When I stop I hear
Please be quiet in room nine.

I hate my bed it's really squeaky.
When I stop moving I hear
Please be quiet in room nine.

I don't like homework it's too hard.
So I stop squirming and I hear
Please be quiet in room nine.

Gemma Mcfarlane (8)
Overdale Junior School

GUINEA-PIGS EAT LOADS

Guinea-pigs eat loads,
Like vegetarian lawnmowers,
They're very small and very round,
Just like half a football.
They go around scavenging for food,
That makes them even rounder,
Give them food every day,
Because you will find it all gone,
If you don't
You will find it
All over the floor with the best bits nibbled.

Alice Pott-Negrine (9)
Overdale Junior School

A DREAM THAT'S NEVER FORGOT

I dreamed I was in a forest one night,
I was nowhere to be seen,
It was gloomy and foggy that night,
The sky was blurred and steamy,
The steam was blowing onto my face,
It was cool like the coolness in the pool,
I was surrounded by scattered leaves,
And suddenly my eyes awakened,
I will never forget that dream,
Ever!

Gurpreet Kaur Deol (9)
Overdale Junior School

SUDDENLY THE DOOR SLAMMED!

Was that the wind? I thought.
There's a creak on the stairs!
I thought I heard soft footsteps.
It was just the cat.

The wind is blowing and howling at me,
The radio is playing spooky music.
Was it the radio?
I feel scared and unhappy,
The tap is dripping, drip, drop, drip,
There's a crash upstairs!
Things are tumbling off the shelf!
Is there something up there?

Chris Pollard (8)
Overdale Junior School

I ONCE SAW A

I once saw a beetle as big as a tiger
with its jaws snapping away, at the driver.
I once saw a tiger as big as a car
that was standing in some tar.
I once saw an elephant as big as a mansion
and it was smashing a mountain!

Martin Sanderson (9)
Overdale Junior School

I THINK MY DOG'S AN ALIEN

I think my dog's an alien,
He's got that kind of face.
He often wishes he could tell me
He comes from outer space.

I believe my dog's an alien,
I think he'll tell me soon.
When he thinks no one's looking,
He dances on the moon.

I know my dog's an alien,
I'm the only one who's seen
That when he's not a furry dog,
He changes to bright green.

Chad Allen (7)
Overdale Junior School

IN THE LAND OF LOOBY LOO

In the land of Looby Loo,
There lived a girl called Troo,
She loved playing tennis,
Her best friend was Glenis,
She lived on board with her crew.

In the land of Looby Loo,
Her feet were stuck with glue,
She couldn't move a bit,
Neither jump nor sit,
And her face was going pale blue.

Luca Jordan (9)
Overdale Junior School

HAPPINESS IS . . .

Happiness is gymnastics and I like going on the beam.
Happiness is to eat chocolate biscuits and ice-cream sweets too.
Happiness is to play the piano and violin.
Happiness is my kittens and my friend's pets.
Happiness is Christmas, birthdays, Easter and Kinder surprises.
Happiness is when my friends come to play, laugh and see my family.
Happiness is going on holiday abroad.
Happiness is Christmas lunch and seeing my dad and his two kittens.

Claire Hannon (9)
Overdale Junior School

LIMERICKS

There once was a lady from Bristol,
Who had a large water pistol,
She squirted her mum,
Right in the tum,
And that made her shout and whistle.

Tom Gill (8)
Overdale Junior School

LIMERICK

There was a young singer called Ellie,
Who wished she could be on the telly,
But on Top of the Pops,
When she took off her socks,
People cried 'Oh, her feet are too smelly!'

Emma Fox (8)
Overdale Junior School

THE JAGUAR

I was walking through the thick bushy ferns,
The mud squelching under my cold and wet feet,
But then my Kayapo guide suddenly turns,
A mighty jaguar lept on him like he's an old seat.

'Run!' he shouts, 'Run,' so that's what I do,
I ran and ran until I found that native man,
I crawled up to him weakly, he was making stew,
He said to me kindly, 'Drink this if you can.'

I swallowed it with difficulty,
It was really nice, was it a dream?
I was right, I woke up to find my mum
Had made me a hot breakfast which was very salty,
I also found on my new blue jeans I had ripped a seam.

Laurie Bennett (9)
Overdale Junior School

I'M WET THROUGH

The water splashes on my face like a massage.
The water drips on my clothes like a slow slug on the wall.
The water freezes my cold fingers like my hand in a freezer.
The water trickles through my hair like rice pudding down my throat.
I'm soaking wet,
I'm soaking wet,
It'll rain tomorrow I bet.

Joe Stewart (9)
Overdale Junior School

WALKING IN THE FOREST

When I walk in the forest
I see light shining
through the dark leaves
and lizards crawling.

When I walk through the forest
I hear monkeys calling,
sloths rustling through the leaves.

When I walk through the forest,
I feel the leaves
and the atmosphere, damp
and steamy around me.
With the forest floor
muddy, squeezy, squelchy,
under my feet.

Belinda Kaur Basra (9)
Overdale Junior School

A WALK IN THE RAINFOREST

I walk alone in the rainforest,
I look around, I see big tall trees,
I hear screeching monkeys,
I see magnificent flowers,
I taste sweet sugar cane,
I come face to face with a jaguar,
I see beams of light falling through the trees,
I walk down a river, I see something,
I think it's a poisonous frog,
It bites me and I'm dead.

Natalie Allen (9)
Overdale Junior School

WALKING THROUGH THE RAINFOREST

Walking through the rainforest
I look up,
I see a beam of light shining straight at me.
I walk along,
When I put my foot on the leaves they make a rustling sound.
I walk along,
The tallest trees look like giant umbrellas.
I walk along the dark and creepy forest,
I hear birds singing.
As I walk along
I see colourful birds
Flying through the forest.
The ground is rough,
Bumpy and hard as I go past.
I see long rooted trees,
I touch the bark gently,
It feels rough, spiky,
And I see trees
Cut down, lying on the forest floor.
I felt like I was having
A wonderful dream
But it is very sad too.

Sarena Kaur Rai (9)
Overdale Junior School

THE STORM

The lightning sparkles like a bright star,
The wind blunders like a wolf's breath,
The fast rain pops and drops like dynamite ready to explode,
The thunder rumbles like a giant jumping.

Prashant K Asher (8)
Rushey Mead Primary School

THE STORM

The lightning is flashing and crashing
like a horrible ghost shaking the roofs.
The thunder is rumbling and stamping
like a fierce giant coming down to eat you.
The wind is howling and scowling
like a lion creeping behind you.
The clouds are whirling and swirling
like a gorilla stuck in a trap.
The rain drips and drops
like a tap dripping and overflowing the house.
The night is scary and black
like a witch trying to grab you.
I am glad I am in bed reading.

Jemini Vaghela (8)
Rushey Mead Primary School

THUNDER!

T hings falling from the roof,
H iding under the table,
U nder the table I am scared,
N ice food under the table,
D elicious scrummy food under the table,
E vil faces in the sky,
R umbling roof, I am scared.

Divya Gosai (7)
Rushey Mead Primary School

THE SCARIEST SKELETON

One scary night some lightning
flashed and dashed, dusha, dusha.
One night at home something
rattled down the stairs, thud, thud,
it was a horrible skull.
It frightened a little girl.
One creepy night a door creaked, creak, creak,
and a boy crawled over the slimy, gungy floor.
One boy was going to bed one night
he heard a clattering noise, clatter, clatter,
there were bones and some footsteps came following behind him,
he didn't like walking up the stairs on his own.

Aarti Sonigra (8)
Rushey Mead Primary School

THE STAR FIGHT

In the dark night the shiny star wakes up
and sees the planets hungrily looking at him.
The star looks at big and small planets and starts to fight.
Crash, bang, smash!
Goes the star.
It sparkled with happiness
after fighting with all the planets.
The star twinkled with happiness like a diamond
and fell fast asleep.

Krupa Jadawji (8)
Rushey Mead Primary School

STORM POEM

In the dark, dark night I went outside,
the wind was swirling and whirling like a ghost,
the rain pops and drops like a mouse squeaking,
the thunder is flashing like a car has crashed
and the puddles are splashing like someone is having a bath.

Sneha Mandalia (8)
Rushey Mead Primary School

STORM

The night is scary and bashing like an angry, strong man.
The clouds are crashing and flashing like a scary monster.
The wind is rumbling and blundering like a lion.
The rain is flickering and stamping like a sharp dice.
The puddles are splashing and flashing like a bird's wings.
The thunder is bashing and lashing like a mental man.
The lightning is bright and lashing like a scary bear.

Manpreet Kaur (7)
Rushey Mead Primary School

STORM

Thunder crashing and banging like a mad giant.
The wind whirring and swirling like a firework.
Clouds spongy and soft like a teddy bear.
Rain pops and drops like ants are falling down.

Dilpesh Varia (7)
Rushey Mead Primary School

THE HUNCHBACK OF BUDGIE LAND

This particular bird is mine - all mine.
Mine to clean,
To feed, to water,
To play, to wash and to love.
I'm convinced he is a strain in
The head.
And this has a knock on effect
On me.
It's like this:
He appeared one day,
Out of nowhere,
Without an invitation.
This was yet another one of Mummy's
Great ideas!
As if I don't have enough to do,
As you imagine.
I'm eight and a half, in full time
Education!
With grown up responsibilities!
But I love my budgie and he loves
Me.

Charlie McKenna (8)
Sacred Heart RC Primary School

FOOD AND DRINK!

Food is yum,
Food is scrum for my tum.
When I eat too much,
Wibble, wobble, wibble, wobble,
Yum, scrum, yum.
I like food, food likes me,
I like eating chips, cake and biscuits.
I like Coca Cola,
Fizzy, tangy, cold Coca Cola,
Straight from the can.
When I take a sip
Its fizzy, tangy, bubbly taste,
Goes round and round in my mouth
And down my throat.
Gulp, gulp, gulp,
Yum!
And it all goes in my
Yum tum tum.

Zeinab Varachia (9)
Shenton Primary School

HOPING

Bright daylight at four,
Hurry home, open the door,
Think of a time when there will be
Daffodils and primroses too.
A bright, light day,
And a spring surprise!

Zaynub Vazifdar (9)
Shenton Primary School

FLOWERS

They're colourful and bright,
What a pretty sight!
Red, purple, yellow and blue,
Orange, green and white too.
You can give a single bunch,
When they dry up they crunch.
I wish someone would give me a rose,
It would have to be red like Rudolph's nose.
Give them to someone you care for,
Once you have them you want more.

Asmaa Patel (9)
Shenton Primary School

SNAILS

A snail slides.
It carries its home on its back.
It leaves tracks on the path.
It's got no nails.
It fails the race.
Snails are slow.
Its shell is as hard as metal.
Its skin is soft, as soft as a cloud.
It's slow.

Anisa Khuresh (8)
Shenton Primary School

ROSES

Roses are red,
Violets are blue,
Sugar is sweet,
And so are you.
The sunshine is shining,
Going to the seaside,
What a lovely thing to do,
Bluebells are sweet,
And so are you.

Aatikha Pandor (7)
Shenton Primary School

SUMMER

The sky is blue,
Trees are green,
Children play,
Flowers grow,
Birds fly,
See them go,
Slurp ice-cream,
Wear short clothes,
Splash in the pool,
The sun shines.

Sunjna Munja (9)
Shenton Primary School

I Saw A Snake . . .

I saw a snake
Who went to the lake.
I saw a snake
Who went to bake a ginger cake.
I saw a snake
Who had a tummy ache.

Reena Nathoo (9)
Shenton Primary School

The Dope

There was a dope called Emma,
Who hit herself with a spanner.
She went to the fair,
And pulled out her hair,
And then she was as bald as bald.

When people found
The hair on the ground,
They nearly died in shock,
So they all had to go to the doc.
Emma went home,
And threw a gnome at a garden fence,
And her mum didn't give her ten pence.

Charlotte Burton (9)
The Hall County Primary School

DANIEL

There was a cocker spaniel
And his name was Daniel.
He had a girlfriend who was a Labrador
And her name was Marador.

Marador went out with Daniel one day
When she saw a male Labrador in the way.
She asked what his name was. He said 'It is Ching.'
Oh! Poor Daniel. Oh! Poor thing.

When Marador got to Ching's home,
Ching gave a little groan,
'What on earth is the matter?'
Marador said 'Can't you see there's a snake in our bed?'

Now Daniel as it may seem,
Had a very cunning scheme.
He got a bone and engraved *To my love*
And then engraved two little doves.

Daniel gave the bone to Marador on the day,
She said 'Thank you,' in a nice way.
Marador and Daniel went together,
While they left Ching sad as a feather.

There was a cocker spaniel
And his name was Daniel,
He had a girlfriend who was a Labrador
And her name was Marador.

Aarti Bilimoria (9)
The Hall County Primary School

DRAKE IS DEAD!

Drake is dead,
No blood or gore.
Just lying in a hammock,
I came to wonder if he even had a scar.

Drake is dead,
No blood or gore.
But he's dead, and that's for certain.
The greatest sailor in the world, his life has actually ended!

Drake is dead,
No blood or gore.
The Spanish never liked him.
On account of when that naughty rogue
Seized the beard of the Spanish king!

Drake is dead,
No blood or gore.
Just there on a sailing ship,
He lived from 1540 to 1596.

Emma Shacklock (9)
The Hall County Primary School